MW01505550

Song of Me

A POETIC MEMOIR

Michelle Oram

© 2024 by Michelle Oram

Song of Me

A POETIC MEMOIR

All rights reserved. No part of this publication may be reproduced, distributed, or transmitted in any form or by any means, including photocopying, recording, or other electronic or mechanical methods, without the prior written permission of the author, except in the case of brief quotations embodied in critical reviews and certain other noncommercial uses permitted by copyright law.

For permission requests, write to the author, addressed "Attention: Permissions Coordinator," 4michelleoram@gmail.com
Orders by U.S. trade bookstores and wholesalers.
Email: 4michelleoram@gmail.com

Manufactured and printed in the United States of America

Book layout by Dana Bree - StoneBear Publishing
Cover illustration by Jerome Plaza
Illustrations from Adobe Stock

ISBN: 978-0-9988930-3-7 Hardback
ISBN: 978-0-9988930-4-4 Paperback
ISBN: 978-0-9988930-5-1 eBook
Library of Congress Control Number: 2024905879

Dedication

To all the people who have listened to the music of my soul
and encouraged me to sing my own song.

To my many students and staff members who have challenged,
taught, and inspired me.

To Dot and Bernadette—one person can truly
make a difference.

To my Pencils Writing group for pushing
me to go beyond.

To Jen Plaza for believing in my gifts
and to my publisher Dana Bree who helped make my
dream a reality.

Here's to future carefree days where peace and acceptance
birth a clear tomorrow.

Testimonials

"Your book is so heartwarming. You capture our hearts with the way you see and approach the world through such vivid descriptions."

— Jen Plaza, Author of *The Legend of Lake Sangre Series*

* * * * *

"I love your honesty, your story and everything you've given and enjoyed with your students over many years. So much resonated with me. This was a read that engaged me immediately. I enjoyed the punctuation of the rhythm (verse/prose). The music."

— Jayne Pink, Movement coach in dance drama, Theatre practitioner.

* * * * *

"This glimpse into your life and the music of nature swept me away. Your way with imagery is especially skillful. I feel so connected to the soul that is your voice."

— Katrien Van Riel, Actor, Musician, Singer, Dancer

* * * * *

"By sharing your vulnerabilities and truths, your growth and your demons, you reveal your mastery of this life journey. And you allow us to face our own journey and be inspired by the hope of finding the omnipresent light of the Infinite Source of Life."

— Janet Vignola, Former Yoga Instructor & dear friend—may she rest in power.

* * * * *

"Michelle is the most inspirational woman I have ever met. She has taught me to love and appreciate all that I have to offer. She has instilled in me ways to not only sing and act, but also ways to live my life in a creative way. Her passion and enthusiasm have helped me grow into the singer, performer, and individual I am today. I am forever grateful for all she has done for me, and all that she continues to do for me."

— Allie Mannarino, Singer and Musical Therapist

★ ★ ★ ★ ★

"Michelle is my mentor. She has taught me so much in the time I've known her. Michelle is a part of my life forever and without her, there's no way I would be where I am today. So, thank you, from the bottom of my heart."

— James Cunningham-Curry, Singer and Songwriter

★ ★ ★ ★ ★

"It is a great joy to see my favorite music teacher, Michelle's profound wisdom and holistic approach to the art of singing, conveyed in these elegant poems. This book is a celebration of the human spirit and the enduring power of music to inspire, uplift, and transform."

— Alex Charles, Music Artist, Songwriter & Producer (*The Ellen Show, Warner Bros, Paramount, Nickelodeon*)

★ ★ ★ ★ ★

"*Song of Me* crawls into deeply personal moments that are universally felt. Poems lift from the prose like a song theatrically blossoms when speaking alone isn't enough. It is a portrait of an artist who champions life, for life. It reminds the reader to listen to the expression of universal love around them and celebrate the glorious symphonic perfection to be heard in the human imperfection of our lives."

— Dan Kazemi, Composer, Orchestrator, Music Director

★ ★ ★ ★ ★

"Michelle Oram was my drama teacher in high school and my first great mentor. Forty some years ago, she taught me about kindness, tenacity and rigor. Her passion for the performing arts, generosity of spirit, boundless sense of humor and sound judgement inform my theatrical practice to this day."

— Darko Tresjnak, Director of plays, musicals, opera, and winner of several awards, including the Tony Award.

Table of Contents

… and the shimmering sounds of our voices
suspend across flickering stars
tears overwhelm our eyes
notes trickle down our cheeks.
The crescent moon beams in silence,
the celestials trumpet
"Let the music take flight,
unravel your heart
to the allurement of your soul."

Prelude Introduction

A teacher can change your life and seal your destiny.
I was blessed
to have that one teacher at an early age.
She taught me
I was enough.

My Vocal teacher helped me grow and become the person
I am today.
When I pushed, or tried to be more by imitating others
my voice felt strained.
When I feared a high note
or doubted a low note
my voice shut down
retreating deep in my throat.

But when I nurtured my voice
and released breath gently
it set free and soared with warmth
energizing my body
vibrating internal organs
releasing tensions built in my everyday life.

Music has been my life jacket
keeping me afloat
in times of trouble.
I've seen life's beauty and strife
wrapped in the notes of many songs
allowing me to drift to faraway secret places.
Sometimes tears melt down my cheeks
as music unlocks the pain in my heart
guiding me down a fresh path
where I can see the promise of a new day.

Music is Poetry

It transforms the way I look at the world.
The gift of life present
through highs and lows of musical
orchestrations rich in melody
as the layering of strings caress woodwinds.
The pounding surf drums
keep the underlying current of my life
moving forward.

I am Music

I sing the notes
of my hound
his rhythmic breath
crescendos
through the ground

The vibe of his jaunt
follows me
as we become one
with the beat
on our daily walk

Through dirt path
grey rock staff layers
our voices
echo the constant
melody of waterfalls

Distant cymbals
of deer brush
slide, glide
crash
in the sun's rays

Soulful
otters dance
the bossa nova
I am music
I sing the songs

of clouds
as they waltz on by
I sing
the dramatic arias
of flowers

The bluesy riffs
bareness of winter
sultry swag of spring
improvised buds of summer
jam through the earth

With a burst of sound
collective voices sing
we are music
we are life
we are one

Tree branches
conduct the rivers'
dynamic symphonic glory
fish jump in high
and low harmony

Hushed murmurs
of birds
drone silences
of evening star
suspensions

Timpani
crickets chime
planets align
grooving to the music
and tempo of us

The finale is autumn
 we expose our souls
 receive
a standing ovation
for our orchestral celebration

I am music
everything is music
everyone who listens
is music
come join in the song

Sans Voce Broken Melodies

I don't recall when I started losing my voice
during my four years at the Conservatory.
Notes blistered away
like a tight pair of stilettos.
I do remember
grueling scales
dissected by a bitter, frustrated performer
now teacher of shattered dreams and dissonant melodies.
Her steel-gray eyes stripped
my songs to just bare notes
as she ordered me to sing
with one tenth of my voice.

"If only, I had your looks," she would moan
as I tried to continue singing Shubert's *Der Tag*.
Each phrase attached to one more
aching sigh of her disapproval
as I tripped on German lyrics
while fighting for breath.
Singing German made me feel
like I was gargling with razor blades
as I choked on consonants.
I once counted six in a row,
unlike French or Italian which glided
through my vocal cords like honey—
their resonances
a facial of pure vibration.
Oh, how I wanted to escape
in Fauré's *Chanson d'Amour*
but here I was, up with the birds
my weekly lesson,
a time of day when most singers are asleep.

I tried to pinch out scales
from the pit of my stomach,
my mouth articulating without sound.
Her berating left me floating on notes
of my mind's criticisms.

Lost on a
dead-end
splinters attach
to my cords
paralyzed
alien
unable to comprehend
what I am doing wrong.
Disparaged eyes
augment my mediocrity
leaving me stripped of song
mocking my existence.
Unable
to move forward
I sit like
a corpse observing
the guests at my funeral
as they mutter
my weaknesses
and shortcomings
to the gods.
I pray someone
will remember
the sparkle of my heart
and how it yearned
to be good
honest and open
leaving nothing
but a song.

My Voice Speaks

Why do you reject me?
Can't you see
my unique possibilities?
Do not abandon me.
I am matched by no other
and will continue to sing
your early morning songs
riding on heartstrings
where I will land
in the valley
of unimaginable potential.
Are you willing to nourish
and unleash my soul?

I dislike old school vocal training,
fast scales racing up and down the piano
tense me in knots.
I fall behind
unable to catch up
begging to slow down
screaming
I am not a piano.

Think of me as a string instrument
a viola to be exact.
I like to warm up slowly—
in long drawn-out resonance.
When I awake
I move faster
in circular motion
connecting vibration
with tone to create sound.
My power is in your breath,
without breath I do not reverberate.
So don't stifle me with criticism,
I will shut down.

I am part of you.
You cannot throw me in a closet
like a flute or clarinet.
There is no escaping me,
I am within you.
How you feel about yourself
reflects my tone.
When you are sick
with an upper respiratory infection
I swell up like a balloon.
Your hormones affect me,
what you eat,
how much you sleep,
even the way you feel
about the world colors my sound.
Nerves cause you to stop breathing
and without breath I cannot exist.

I do love to stretch in the warmth
of a cup of tea sweetened with honey.
And when you sing from your heart
and dismiss
the restrictive voices of your mind,
I am unstoppable.

For me to thrive—
embrace me,
sour notes and all
until I grow inspired
to unleash my greatness.

So, practice every day
until it becomes second nature.
Wear your music like
a worn-out T-shirt.
Think outside the box.

Care, love and be passionate
until your commitment
is infectious
and you find your exclusive voice,
transforming
into your own best teacher.

Overture Opening Night

I was awakened
by a moonbeam last night
It reached for me
through my window

I put my hand out
and was spotlighted
in silken blue chiffon

embraced with applause
it cheered
"You are not done,
you are just beginning"

The smokey indigo
curtain closed
I waited for it to reopen
perhaps an encore
of *Tell me more*
and then
the stage went dark

Concertos French Hill

"Remember, don't talk to strangers"
my mother called out drowsily from her bed.
I don't know why I wasn't terrified
to walk the three-quarter-mile hike to school
but there I was, a little six-year-old (well, maybe not so little)
with big brown eyes, pixie-cut auburn hair
excited, feeling a bit grown up.

When I was a kid
we walked to school,
walked home for lunch—
walked back to school
and walked home again.
There were no carpools in the early 60s
and you had to live more than a mile
from school to take a bus.
Our parents and grandparents survived
the Great Depression so no one ever complained
about walking a few miles, especially on a full stomach
unless you wanted the "When I was a kid" lecture.

French Hill was a middle-class neighborhood
with fatigued, average, two-family houses
in need of attention.
Most of the inhabitants were of Quebec stock
and everyone spoke French.
The savory aromas of home cooking
greeted me each morning as proud homemakers
smiled and waved "bonjour."
I, always, smiled back
while preoccupied in song.

On my walk one day, I stopped mid-hum
and there she appeared. Her eyes desolate,
lacked melody, in search for a mate
craving the trust of someone who might listen.
Do you want to be my friend?
She responded by giving me her paw
and a slippery, gentle kiss.
I will call you Little Fond.
She was small, with a black pointy nose
and blonde foxlike coat.
Little Fond was one of many dogs escorted out the door
every morning after breakfast
and let in the house at dinner time, much like us kids.
No one ever knew exactly where we were
and like most mutts, no one cared.
If we were in the neighborhood
our parents knew we were safe, and we'd better be home
for dinner to avoid a spanking.

The long hill slid down to school
carpeted with maple, chestnut, and elm trees.
Rabbits nibbled on grass, all ablaze
from the sun melting the early morning frost.
I never was alone.

I could always find a lonely dog or needy cat
to befriend and talk to.
There seemed to be an overabundance of critters
everywhere, paving the way to my destination.
I became the Pied Piper of French Hill.

One day, as I reached the summit of the hill
I realized I was being serenaded.
I followed the sound and there he was
a cherry-red cardinal, chirping in delight
basking in rays of sunshine
feeling secure in the branches
of an old majestic oak tree.
I froze in his sacredness, lost in the beauty of his song.
And then, as if his notes opened a magical, sparkling
storybook
I noticed a wonderland of birds all around me
finches—all colors of the rainbow, robins, sparrows
blue jays, warblers, wrens, red-winged blackbirds
titmice, crows, pigeons, mourning doves.
Nature's morning concerto engulfed me.
I looked up at the crystal blue sky,
tears of gratitude trickled down my cheeks.

From that day on, walking to school
was a musical theater escapade
melodic crumbs tracking the ups and downs of my path.
My entourage of animal friends
scraggly mutts—all different sizes
led by Little Fond
followed me to and from school every day.
The uniqueness of each bird's song
intrigued me as I stopped to listen along the way.

I learned when you sing to a bird, it answers back.
The cardinals had the prettiest voices
and loved to show off their vocal runs.

But there was one bird, always hidden
who tried so hard to sing a melody.
It swayed between two sour notes
creating monotone dissonance.
The other birds tried to drown it out
but it kept blasting louder and louder,
determined and oblivious to all around.

Because of my love of birds, I dreamt about being a tree.
Maybe an oak tree
so strong and able to withstand the elements of time,
the frosty cold of winter, hurricanes of fall,
scorching heat of summer,
the promise of buds in spring.

Or perhaps, a juniper tree
tall and majestic, with lacy green crocheted branches
able to fan and shelter, never shedding my leaves.

Yes, I believe, a juniper tree
is what I'd truly love to be.

My aromatic branches spiraling
toward the sun's rays
tickled by the marvels of a new day.
The roots of ancient years past
buried deep in the earth's crust
connecting me to all above and below
as I would peer through teary clouds
rocking and cradling the many birds
perched on my branches,
while they sang and delighted me
with their endless songs of happiness and woe.
Rustling leaves blowing in the wind
added harmony to the bird's constant melody.
And I would be blessed to be surrounded
by so many songs of splendor.

Lullabies Music in Nature

Forest brook
whispers
pacify my heart
rockabye rhythms
cradle me to sleep

lullabies of crickets,
cicadas and tree frogs
soothe
my soul
in peaceful slumber

I awake
to a symphony of birds
in celebration of a new day
I peer out my sun cast window
and sing to a chickadee

little bird
can you hear my song?
little bird
can you hear my plea…
I have journeyed to and fro

in pursuit of melody
understood
my notes reach out
upon silent ears
little bird, hear my heartsong
do not take flight.

Nature's orchestrations have always
awoken me at dawn,
as I would join in the melodies
of the sun's rays shining
through my bedroom window.
The symphonic chirpings
would echo through my backyard
highs and lows
delicate and robust
as an abundance of birds
would sing their early morning songs
in celebration of a new day.
I would watch them
so delicate and fragile
flying, trusting the velocity of the wind.
Birds understand the importance
of silence and space
when conjuring up a melody.
They taught me how to listen.
And how sometimes life's mistakes,
like melodies,
repeat themselves over and over
 until we learn a new melody
 a new beginning
 a new song.

Bel Canto My First Voice Teacher

In third grade
an exotic
Hungarian woman
with a lustrous thick accent
coached me in vocal training.
I think her name was Natasha
or maybe I just called her that
because she reminded me of Natasha Fatale—
Boris Budanov's partner in crime
in *The Rocky and Bullwinkle* cartoons
I so loved.

Smells of fried garlic and onions
wafted off her body
and perfumed her house
during my lesson each week.
It never bothered me.
I love the smell of garlic.
I find to this day
it really does open
my nasal passages.

I got lost in her cluttered
Victorian flowered
living room
framed in lace curtains,
stuffed with porcelain
and crystal knickknacks.
Piles of music invaded
the top of her antique studio piano.

Natasha was a famous opera singer
or so I believed,
with a dark villainous

mezzo-colored sound.
Her voice
reminded me of Maria Callas,
her accent and physical stature
Natasha Fatale.
Her raven eyes,
coarse jet-black hair,
thick sinister eyeliner,
and sky-blue eye shadow
cast a spell on me
inspiring me
to sing with discipline and passion.

Some of the repertoire I sang with Natasha
felt a bit forbidden and grownup
for a nine-year-old—
lyrics of kissing
every day of the week
but *Never on a Sunday*
as I shook my giggly hips
to a sexy bossa nova beat.

I will forever cherish
my first voice teacher
who taught me
to dream
and get lost
Somewhere Over the Rainbow.

Sanctus Hymns — My Gift

Floating, weightless, billowy
filling my soul with life
a white light illuminates
my body's core
discovering sustenance
and peace as I let go
of sorrows and tribulations.
I inhale the power of trust.
My voice like the tail of a kite
follows the path of each exhale.
I release and surrender
to new possibilities,
my heart celebrates
in song.

I knew at a young age,
I was different and had a special gift—my voice.
Singing in Church with rains of conviction
my heart poured out to the heavens.
I went to mass every day
at Saint Mary's French Parochial School.
Our prayers were in French
songs in English and Latin.
My voice echoed and bounced off stone edifices,
riding on smoky waves of frankincense and myrrh,
as the statue of the blessed Mary, hands outstretched
heard my voice and smiled.
I was never embarrassed to sing my heart out to God.
I felt the mightiness of each note release from my soul.
I considered singing sacred because when I sang,
I could transform and move people in a positive way.
And most important,
when I sang,
there was no fighting.

I had solos in school shows starting at age six, yet what
inspired me to write, direct, and perform took place at our
family's dinner table each night.
My parents insisted we eat every morsel of food on our plates
and told us daily, "Remember all the starving children in
India." Oh, how I wished I could send those starving children
my instant mashed potatoes, liver, and canned peas. I came
up with the idea to have a show every few weeks, charge
admission, and give the money to all the needy children of
the world.
Back in the 60's, five dollars was all you needed to provide
shots, food, and clothing for a famished child for a whole year,
or so the TV commercials told us.
So, I took a king-size sheet and transformed our outside
stand-up clothesline into a rehearsal tent and went to work
auditioning neighborhood kids for my bimonthly variety

shows. My father grilled sausages and onions and sold hot dogs and soda pop (called tonic in Boston), and my mother sold some of her artwork. In a short time at the age of eleven, I was the mother of fifty mission babies.

The show I recall most was *The Flying Nun*. Of course, I played Sister Bertrille, the role made famous by Sally Field. I had her bangs, voice, and the gargantuan apple tree that I could climb, sing, and appear from. Perhaps it was my intimate connection with birds that made me think I could fly. I spent countless hours waiting for the right wind to come and sweep me away, so I could glide with my birdie friends.

I truly believed I had the soul of a bird.

I was honored when the nuns asked me to direct, produce, and act in my elementary school fundraiser, which I decided would be *Mary Poppins*. I cast myself as Bert. It only made sense as a director: I was the best dancer and had the highest energy level. I gave the part of Mary Poppins to my sophisticated friend Maureen. Her mother was a great seamstress and helped us with all the costumes. The nuns sold popcorn in brown paper bags and apple juice in dixie cups.

It was a fun experience for all.

The next fundraiser was *The Wizard of Oz*. I got to play my dream role, Dorothy. I will never forget my classmates' dazed faces, and the thunderstruck looks of the nuns when they discovered I added contemporary pop songs to give the script my own voice. Of course, "Somewhere Over the Rainbow" was still in, but Scarecrow was now singing Engelbert Humperdinck's hit "Please Release Me," and Tin Man's big solo was now Tony Bennett's "I Left My Heart in San Francisco." I thought it was out-of-the-box brilliant! It set a precedent for years to come.

Whether a song, play or musical, I was always compelled to make it my own.

Diminuendo No One Ever Knew

J grew up in a time when no one aired their dirty laundry; what took place within the family stayed in the family. Your family's income or personal matters was none of your damn business. There was a code of conduct that didn't allow you to question your elders. You were punished (spanked) if you criticized your teacher. You were taught to honor your parents. It was a sin to say or think anything negative about them. If you did disobey, the strap was an acceptable punishment.

Because my mother slept a lot and got hysterical if we woke her, I seldom had friends visit.

"You kids better not disturb your mother, she is very sick and needs her sleep", the family doctor scolded us after making a house call.

My mother was always ill, sometimes for weeks at a time. At age nine it was my job to keep my younger brothers and sister occupied and quiet or I got punished. I attempted to play games in the basement to keep my siblings happy; Monopoly, Checkers, Fish, Rummy, War, even Bridge. Then, when everyone got bored, we went outside and played house, school, or veterinarian hospital—games in which hopefully there was no fighting.

No one ever knew
how much I cried
myself to sleep at night.

No one ever heard
the crash of broken glass
buried in my dreams.

No one ever saw
the violent outbursts
and drunken brawls.

No one would ever believe
my mother heard raging voices
singing to her paranoia.

Or that my father
losing his way home
drowned his fears in bars.

No one ever knew
how much I tried to glue
the broken pieces back together.

People believed I was born into
the perfect All-American family.

As I sang and danced my way
into their hearts on French Hill.

They knew of a middle class
hard working functioning household.

People knew my father was
a chef and my mother a nurse.

Aromas of pies and baked goods
were sold at my house every week.

People would be shocked
when the beautiful couple divorced
after 12 years of marriage.

And watched as our bloodline
spiraled into darkness.
No one, could pick up the pieces,
not even me.

Chorale My Music Family

The "A" Building was
a modern, rectangular edifice
magically transformed
by continual layers of music.
Closet-sized practice rooms
housed arpeggiated vocal warm-ups,
Broadway and classical art songs.
The band room across the hall
fought for attention
as orchestral groups, chamber ensembles, jazz combos
and marching band members practiced.
In the choral room on Thursdays
the fifties group be-bopped to the sounds
of *Heartbreak Hotel* and *Chantilly Lace*,
Concert Choir embraced
Fauré's *Requiem* on Mondays and Wednesdays,
the Madrigal group sang with purity
A Capella Gregorian chants on Tuesdays.
Our 140-person award winning chorus
rehearsed in the auditorium—
the only place big enough to accommodate us.

Our leader Mrs. DiDomenico,
queen mother to us all
stood a little under five feet tall,
her cushioned frame and silver-sparkled hair
pulled back in a clip,
resembled the matronly Beatrice Potter
hedgehog character Mrs. Tiggy-Winkle,
dark-framed cat-like glasses
glided to the tip of her button nose.
And when she gave you the *look*—trains stopped.

If we didn't like a piece of music
she would reply,
"You'll learn to love it!"
We craved our little maestro's attention,
approval, and love.
One of her favorite sayings was
"Do as I say, not as I do,"
as she puffed away
a pack of cigarettes a day.
We loved her so much
the cloud of smoke
would not deter us
from compressing like sardines
into her tiny office at lunchtime.
Mrs. Di knew the influence she had
over us and was always there
when we needed to talk
or a shoulder to cry on.

Two choral experiences
during this time
had a major impact on me and
changed my life while
securing my destiny—
Randall Thompson's
Ye Shall Have a Song
from *The Peaceable Kingdom*
and *Choose Something Like a Star,*
from *Frostiana,*
a tribute to Robert Frost.

Our voices ignited
by the heavens
dissolved in magnitude
while we breathed and sang as one.

Body hairs overwhelmed
by lustrous eight-part harmonies
awe-inspired tears trilled
down my cheeks
notes and melodies
vibrated my heart.
Opening my eyes
to many things
we can rely on in this world—

the sun as it crescendos
and decrescendos
as birds celebrate in song

the strength of a tree
branches modulating
in bluesy gospel tones

the clouds suspended
in the ocean sky
melodically drifting on by

the moon peering down
on vast concertos
of the earth's shadows

Music the everlasting bond
connected our souls
and Mrs. Di inspired us
to follow our hearts' footprints
leading us
down a path of enlightenment
where we were all one
as our voices reached for the stars.

Our music program became
one of the best in the state
because of Dorothy DiDomenico.
She was the mother I never had.
Her love of music
branded my soul
forever changing
how I felt
about life and the world.
Connecting me
with everything
and everyone.

I knew
I would try to recreate
these experiences
for myself and others
for the rest of my life.

Da Capo My Dad

Blue and white
cop by day
chef by night,
as mom insisted
on financial security,
he would sing
no more in nightclubs.

And when I was old enough to walk
my dad had me crooning to
"Friends, neighbors, countrymen,"
anyone we'd meet on the street.
"This is my daughter,
a straight-A student at Saint Mary's.
Sing something for them, sweetie"—
swallowing my awkwardness,
I would, on command,
like an obedient pup,
sing whatever popped
in my head
my dad's smile revealed his pride.

Edward Joseph grew up
during the depression,
as a little boy he helped
support his family of ten,
selling magazines
baking doughnuts.
He never finished school.
"When your dad was a little boy,
he paid for all my piano lessons,"
my Aunt Katie loved to tell me.

He cooked dinners fit for a king,
while he sang to his treasured jazz albums
Tony Bennett's, *I Left My Heart in San Francisco*,
Nat King Cole's *Unforgettable*,
taking breaks to imitate Jackie Gleason—his favorite entertainer.
He resembled Gleason,
his bulging, dancing eyes
yelling "To the moon, Alice or and away we go"—
a boastful, stout man,
a true performer at heart.
I loved to stand on his feet
as we glided across the kitchen floor,
like Ginger Rogers and Fred Astaire.
My Boston terrier, Teddy, watched
head tilted, tail wagging.

Dad's dancing wasn't limited to the kitchen.
He had a reputation
as the dancing traffic cop,
soft-shoeing his way through
the monotony of directing traffic
from seven to three,
then came home fixed us a snack,
put on his floppy white hat
and became the infamous Chef Edward.
He worked
at the Marlborough Country Club on weekends,
and during the week in our basement home-bakery,
sometimes from four in the afternoon
until two in the morning.
Aromas of homemade pies,
fig and date nut bars
put me to sleep.
Pots of dirty cemented lemon and apple pie filling
greeted me to be washed when I got up.
One of my chores as his helper.

My father was no saint.
Cooking helped conceal
his drinking habit.
Not always a happy drunk
when challenged
he became belligerent.
I awoke many nights
to hollering, slapping
dishes crashing.
My parents fought nonstop
especially when Mom got home
from work at the hospital
and found Dad passed out
in the living room
cigarette in hand.

I learned to exercise
my mind to feel light
as a feather
my body drifting up to the ceiling,
steering my way out of my bedroom
through the kitchen, and effortlessly
out the window,
where I spread my wings like an eagle
and soared back to sleep.

I have been flying and soaring
in my dreams
for as long as I can remember,
cherishing the feelings
of weightlessness and freedom,
as I escaped battlegrounds.

Art Songs When I was little

*W*hen I was little
Mom
I spent hours
watching you paint.
Lost in your art,
an English countryside
Little Boy Blue petting a lamb
his mother—a beautiful, statuesque woman
with long wavy brown hair
blowing in the wind,
wearing a white
chiffon gown with a teal sash
yearning to be free.

When I was little
you knitted, hand-braided rugs,
wallpapered, and sewed.
I was in awe of all you did,
as I tried to learn
craving
your approval.

When I was little
you cut and permed my hair
steel sharp bobby-pin waves, rag curls
French pixie cuts
with straight bangs that disappeared
into my scalp.
I would plead, *Can't I let my hair grow long?*
But you look so French
with your cute Parisian haircut!

When I was little
You would erupt
uncontrollably
into hyena hysterics,
making us all join in the pack.
You played tennis, golfed,
and swam always needing
your twelve hours of sleep
so, you could function.
You fed on male adoration
and knew the flirting games
of the 40s black-and-white movies
the tilt of the head,
seductive gaze,
how to look disinterested,
and laugh teasingly
with your inviting Cheshire cat smile
perfect white teeth
so big
they made your lips vanish.

When I was little
I loved when you blasted
boxed cassettes
of Barbra Streisand, Judy Garland,
and Glen Campbell on our stereo.
I would knit or do my embroidery
as I listened,
sometimes unleashing
emotions of happiness and sadness.
I felt the power of your music
the many feelings
each song conjured up within me.
Music transformed you
and brought peace and love.
I hoped one day my voice
would do the same.

Pop Songs My Radio

The many nights in bed,
my black-and-white angora cat, Tootsie,
melodically purred in my ear,
expressing her love and devotion.
Some people get lost in books,
I always got lost in music.
The numerous channels
of my radio
lead me down new tracks
sometimes dark and painful
like a torch song;
sometimes high-spirited
making me break out in dance,
swinging and tapping.
Music so lush my heart
suspended in time
as I burst out in tears
of delight and anguish simultaneously.
My radio filled with musical surprises
The Sounds of Silence,
How High the Moon, Alfie,
Walk the Line
all I had to do was turn the knob
and presto,
a new tune would fill the air
whenever I desired.

My black transistor radio
was my best friend
for most of my youth
as my mother fell deeper
into her delusional
Sleeping Beauty world
where she dreamt
of her lost Prince Charming,
seesawing between doctors
she should have married
or remaining a nun.
I never should have left the convent.
Mother Superior said I would never be happy
in the outside world, she would lash out at us.
My father answered with his fists,
as I, powerless
struck by fear,
hammered my head
against dark
wood paneling
until the fighting stopped.

When Mom wasn't working
part-time,
she was home
and I was punished
in bed most nights by six
her piercing green catlike eyes
turned my heart to stone.
Maybe she wanted to be alone
and didn't want me watching TV
while she slept in the living room.
"You have a smirk on your face."
What's a smirk?

"Go to your room," she would holler!
Her chapped, slapped
enraged face snapped
as I ran into my room
eyes slammed shut.
At age seven
I had no clue what the word smirk meant.
Did I look like a jerk?
Were my eyes berserk?
In the shadows of my room,
I would lurk
and pray for redemption.
I tried to be my mother's helper

I scrubbed and scrubbed
until the porcelain
chipped away
from my heart

I cleaned dirt from
dark secret places
ashes scattered in coffee
her pasty, broken, runny
eggs prepared me
for life's journey
as I tried to pass

invisible from her wrath
sculpted on the sofa
once with paint brush
in hand, no more

As slumber erases
all dreams
nightmares multiply
replacing day with night

and night with day
pills get popped, dropped
adding to the decay
I pick up the pieces

I am my mother's helper

Then I would run to my room,
shut the door
drown my tears
to the songs
on my radio.

Decrescendo Waiting for the Thaw

I wish I could cry away
the guilt
of a frozen heart
torn, beaten
suffocated
by your schizophrenic inferno
but the scars
burn deep
The gangrene
of my frostbitten
childhood
rots away
lost
happy memories
no matter how much
I try
the paralysis
of my life
with you
won't wear off
unlike pop songs
you belted out
to your favorite
records
in the living room
before you slinked out
to a local bar
your feral green eyes
bloodshot and tainted
as you craved to purr
in the arms
of strangers
while I waited
for you to slither

your way back home
I took over
your motherly duties
caring and feeding
my younger siblings
with tears of guilt
for not being
the mother
they so deserved
So today
on your birthday
I plant a garden
of lily-of-the-valley
your favorite scent

I listen to birds
that once soothed
your drunken demons

I wait for the thaw
of my frozen heart
to sing the notes
of your favorite song
The Way We Were

Fermata Life on Hold

I love to play
hooky
from life
pajama days
brush my teeth
maybe not
hidden in my barricade oasis
bunked on my sofa
mug of tea by my side
book and pen in hand
fire singing with delight
all seems right.
Fresh snow descending
cleanses
frozen lake muck
from a world filled with debris
a tunnel of evergreens
encompasses me
securing my path
to nothingness.
My life unfolds
with the flow
of the nearby dam
distant drones
winds hum,
planes strum
refrigerator moans
steel pipe groans
then
stillness so quiet
I can hear the blood
swirl in my veins.

Flurries dance
in constant motion.
The rhythm
of my contentment
cradles a blizzard
of blissful memories
avalanching
my insecurities
leaving behind ashes
of yesterday's tears.
I embrace
the frozen numbness
of my childhood
the white pearls
of my mother's smile
her forest green eyes
blinded with despair
her irrational cutting words
in search of meaning
her highs and lows
as winter confetti
attaches to sun glistened
sprinkles of time.

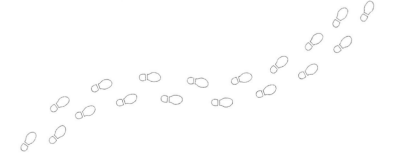

Reflections in the Snow

Sometimes I walk down
a path
where all I can hear
is the frozen crunch
of dead leaves

I get lost in a dense fog
of *if only*
disoriented with
my mind's inadequacy
I sit by a trickling brook

My life swirls downstream
against outcast stones
icicles of pain
seesaw with ripples
of happiness

I look to the sky
laced silken misty
spun webs of snow
begin to spiral
in every direction

I surrender
to the downy ground
tears melt
the cold storm
off my cheeks

Frosted with forgotten
childhood memories
I stretch
my once angelic arms
sculpting snow angels

My imagination
sings and flies
on doves' wings
my youthful dreams return
cleansed and refreshed

Snowflakes cover
many troubled
yesterdays
retrieving collections
of magical domino scenes
from my youth

tongues stuck
to glistening icicles
building snowmen
sledding down hills
picnics in ice castle
fortresses, I the queen
carving safe havens
in blocks of white
sheltered from
my parent's brawls
frozen forever
in my heart

What hides beneath
the fluffy blankets
of maternal snow
carpeting my yard
once gardens

flavored with lavender
today a tundra
where birds tuck away
nuts and berries
from yesterday's harvest

now the seeds of spring
are protected by nature's purge
embracing tomorrow
with blossoms
of hope

Étouffée Whisperings

Fleeing on a hot summer's day to LaBelle's dairy farm,
I ordered a creamy butter pecan ice cream cone—
my favorite.
My mother just kicked my dad out of the house
and there was talk of divorce.
The thought of being the only divorced family in a devout,
French-Catholic neighborhood made me feel dirty.
The church condemned divorce,
a mortal sin,
never to be forgiven.
We would be denounced by our church:
a building where I spent six years of my life —
praying, singing, learning, even cleaning.
Would my parents burn in hell for this mortal crime?
How could I face my friends?
I felt numbly disgraced.
Soon, the whispers on French Hill mimicked
the downfall of my home.

Shamed rainfall
Church gossip
drenched in the stench
of judgment
manure pasted flatulence
thick in despair
permeates air

Did you hear
who would have thought
I can't believe it
poor kids
I heard—

What did you expect
her mom used to be a nun
She rejected her vows
now the sacrament of marriage

Caught in Adam and Eve's
stained
menstruated guilt
bar hopping lows
as the family leaves
to escape the whisperings
on French Hill

I was dizzy with fear.
And then —
I spotted on the barn-red picnic table
a little chickadee, lost in slumber.
I inched my way to study the bird,
its yellow beak and fluffy mosaic design were so intricate.
My heart stopped
when the delicate creature let me pick it up.
It opened its watery eyes and seemed
to melt my shame away.
Things would be okay.
Some things were meant to be.
God has a plan, and I am a part of that plan.

I opened my hands and watched the bird fly—
leaving me spellbound.

Scherzo Dancing as fast as I can

I've spent many years making people believe I come from the perfect All-American family, until age sixteen when my world shattered.

Deep in sleep I drift upon birds' wings.
Awakened by stars bursting through clouds
into an ocean of chaos.

I let out a piercing, strangled scream
run from room to room, in shadows
trying not to step on broken glass.

Racing down the blackish highway
clothed in my tattered summer nightshirt,
I disappear into obscurity.
My heart mangled
paralyzed
like a frightened little bird
hiding from a starved raven.

A giant monstrous shadow
approaches and flashes a blinding light
piercing my burning bloodshot eyes.

There is no bird to be heard.
There is no song to be sung.
I am alone
and no longer dreaming.

"Are you ok? Why are you hiding in this bush at 3am?" The steely police officer inquired.

"My mother broke all the windows in the house and told me she would kill herself if I did not leave immediately.
"Where do you live?"

"Down the highway across from the prison farm," I mumbled without feeling.

"You'll have to come in and file a report. Do you have anyone you can stay with tonight?" he asked with pitying eyes.

"I have a friend I can call who lives in Concord."

And it was from that point, at age sixteen, I was no longer living with my mother. Even worse, everyone would soon know I did not come from the perfect All-American family, a role I had perfected for years.

My secret would be out and the looks of pity which I despise would cast my way. I was not an injured bird. I did not want anyone to feel sorry for me. I just wanted to keep up a normal façade by going to school, singing, and performing in shows.

A few days later, school counselors along with my high school music teacher set up a meeting with me and my mother to evaluate the situation.

My mother was on the defensive and made me out to be an evil child.

"You don't know her!"

The hate in her piercing green eyes cut deep. She proceeded to tell her side of the story and tried to justify her actions, while making me out to be a horrific out-of-control teen.

There was no apology, no words of kindness or love. She was a caged animal, and I was the predator who threatened her life. Sitting there in the office dazed in disbelief I wondered what I had ever done to have her hate me so much.

I tried so hard to be the perfect child—I cleaned, cooked, got straight A's. I didn't do drugs, alcohol, or even smoke cigarettes. How could my mother not love me?

It was evident to all that I would not be returning home.

To this day, within me lies a darker side of the rainbow, shadowed with doubt, where my mind questions my heart and wonders why I was never loved by my mother. My eclipsed side is always trying to find my way back home detouring down gloomy hurtful paths.

I could never despise or resent my mom.

How can you resent
clouds
on a rainy afternoon
or a plant dying
from too much sun
and not enough water.
We accept these things
as part of our everyday lives.

But what about a mother
who cannot remember
your birthday?
A mother who can barely care
for her own needs.
You can never expect anything
except
the endless void of a stranger
who is incapable.

At a very young age I decided that if I lived every day as if it were my last and filled every minute with an activity—I would never suffer from the mental illness that plagued my mother. Thus, the name of this chapter of my life—SCHERZO which is a musical term meaning *a fast happy dance.*

Yes, I have spent my life dancing as fast as I can.

Voce My Inner Teacher

Within me
a monument of books
from ancestors past
buried deep in my soul.

All I must do is download
each beat of my heart
to unlock the pages,
sit and read
mind open
eyes thirsting.

Every chapter reveals
all I have been taught.
I am a life of first and second drafts,
constant edits and revisions.
A published author
of many volumes.

And just as the sun
leads way
into the unknown
at the end of each day
so too, I must kindle
the teacher within
to launch
the bestseller
I am.

A teacher's job is to help the student go beyond their comfort zone through trial and error. There must be a relationship of trust and deep respect as the teacher builds a safe playground where the student can grow, be challenged, and most important, take risks. A playground where the student can explore and let go of all fears, delve into the unknown of the sacred instrument—the voice.

It is time for me to become my own best teacher.

Autumn Cleanse

A hodgepodge of color
woven through
blocked evergreens
embroidered branches
stitched with multi-colored threads
strip away
sharp, bitter rains
of yesterday's
sunbaked blossoms
moldy moss
clings to bark
like trophies
never to be forgotten
tapestry mountains
piece a new path
distant memories
wrinkles of time
make room
for a new tomorrow

Deep within me, lies a unique jewel that cannot be scratched. To connect with this jewel, I must practice the art of going beyond my thoughts to a place where I am accepted, cherished, and loved unconditionally.

To be true to my voice, I must treat it with reverence, a sacredness that can only be found in the dwelling temple of my heart. My heart does not judge or condemn. It honors the musical notes of my voice rooted in my heart, where singing becomes a prayer, a meditation, a celebration of the soul.

I must make each song an offering, dedicate a song to someone or something, and watch as my heart opens and frees my blocked mindset. Sometimes I find my mind and heart are at war–

You see trials and tribulations
I see blessings and gratitude
You see pain from a broken heart

I see a heart happy to love
You resent all who have wronged me
I resent no one who has made me stronger

You see all the reasons why not
I see all the vast possibilities.
You say . . . if only
I say . . . whatever
My mind sees the glass half-empty
My heart sees the glass half-full

No two voices are alike. My voice has many colors that are highlighted by my unique emotional experiences. Each voice is distinctive and has its own personal journey.

Music is not all technical. When I make it so, I begin to critique every sound, as if the world was black and white or pass and fail. When I remove the judgment of my mind, I am open and free, enabling myself to sing without fear of criticism.

Singing is breath, focus and sound.
When I speak, I do not examine the sound of every word
that comes out of my mouth.
When I sing, I question all that can go wrong.

I have loved singing ever since I was a baby,
performing and sharing songs for anyone who would listen.
When did it turn to self-criticism?
Does self-awareness make me shut down?
When did I start being afraid
to have fun and play with songs?
I must try to tame the perfectionist within me.

Perfection is the ice princess enemy
of creativity,
who lives in a crystal tower.
The walls of her mind are built
from doubt.
Kept prisoner by her flaws
she dwells in an abyss
of uncertainty,
clinging to the familiar,
never venturing to take risks,
her heart begins to decay.
The glimmer of what once was,
what could have been
devours her soul.

Perfection is a one-way street to nowhere. It's time to let my heart lead the way to the teacher within—so I may see, not just my voice, but everything around me with new eyes.

I've made a career
holding
onto the impossible.
Cemented
in past rejections
afraid
of change
unable
to surrender
to the winds of fall.
Oblivious
to the array of color
blossoming
glory
to make room
for a new
story.
The bare pallet
winter provides
allows
spring to
sing
a new song
off the beaten path.

A s I walk home on this autumn day, I breathe in all I see. The ordinary, everyday bushes and trees, I took for granted just hours ago, are now ablaze with color. What was once commonplace is now a work of art, a creation of uniqueness. The sunny yellow and deep burnt-orange foliage against an indifferent, dull palette sky, makes me realize that no matter how gray a day I might be having, all I must do is go outside, stand still, and awaken in the blessedness all around me.

And just like the leaves of fall,
maybe I can let go of all that is wrong,
and concentrate on all that is right.

Dynamics Sibling Relationships

Snow crystals
kaleidoscope
shape and design
tumbling from clouds
exposed
to fluctuating temperatures.
They share the same history
in their making
yet, no two snowflakes
are alike.
Much like siblings born
into the same family,
each singing different
unique melodies.

My parents had four kids in four years.
I am the eldest.

My Brother Ed

Fearless
he sails down diamond
ski slopes of Lake Tahoe,
icicle beard glistening
against a backdrop
of ocean blue sky,
as he escapes
into the mountains
of his heart.
A builder of dreams
with the gift of gab
and the vision of a hawk.

Capable of seeing
the souls of others,
connecting common
threads of all
with the aromas
of his cooking.

A major league ball player
able to catch and run
with whatever life
throws his way,
stealing home plate
never striking out.
A devoted husband,
his no-frills temple
is his home and family,
whom he will protect
from the mudslides
of tomorrow.

My brother Ed, my Irish twin, found his escape in sports and rebelled against school. Back in the sixties you were either smart or stupid. There were no such things as learning disabilities, just simple branding which crippled the mind.

My brother Ed and I have travelled down different paths most of our lives but we always end up full circle.

My Brother David

My brother David was different. His green frog-like eyes attracted the wonder of small helpless creatures; snakes, bugs, snails, as he climbed and hung from the tallest trees, looking down at the world, never quite fitting in, and he …stuttered.

Stutter, stutter
afraid to mutter
trying to fit in
not knowing
where to begin.

Stutter, stutter
afraid to mutter
hiding shame
under rocks
behind blocks
capture snails
pets in pails
hide under pillow
sleeping willow.

Silent screams
awaken your
dreams,
you gasp
a muted yell
no escape
from hell,
you drown
in a frown.
Stutter, stutter
afraid to mutter
all the kids laugh
break you in half,
wish you had a gun.

You befriend snakes
wrap
yourself in leather
words glide
light as a feather.

With no mistakes
you hiss
your tormentors
now feared
less scared.
As you
Stutter, stutter
searching for acceptance
drunken words
from your father
who shakes his head
in *disapproval.*

David spent half of his life astray. In his later years his health
revolted, leaving him homebound, forcing him to connect to
his art. Today he paints ocean scenes, mountains, and birds.

My Sister Lisa

My sister could do no wrong in our mother's eyes.
Lisa, tall and slender with a black stallion mane,
was a daredevil, jumping over hurdles, cantering, and
galloping the many prize-winning horses she rode daily.
"Your sister Lisa is nothing like you. She is like me,
adventurous," our mother loved to point out.
As I, with my auburn pixie, big boned, fearful, responsible,
the Suzy homemaker who loved to cook and sew
took on all the responsibilities of the world.

Lisa, with delicate features hid under long silky hair,
her body starved for control
and by junior high became
a whirlwind of rebellion.
She was the youngest,
deserted by her siblings
who fled from the nest
to save themselves.
She followed our mother's trail of drunkenness.
Every drunk wants a drinking buddy
and my sister took on that role very early in her teens and
struggled most of her life with the demons of pain, anger,

and terror our mother planted in her youth.

My sister left this world in the spring at age forty-three,
I was by her side,
her body ballooned with intestinal toxins.
The tubes around her rolled in a ball like skeins of yarn.
Nurses and doctors tried to pump endless IV fluids in her.
Drowning in heavy tears
I watched her body grasp onto life support
while her mind battled to be set free,
like a wild horse fighting to be unrestrained.
I tried to hum life into her withered body
as I clung to her hand searching for a beat of her heart,
singing every lullaby I knew.

Lisa died from a fatal form of pneumonia. When I phoned
our mother with the news, sounding battered and frail she
quivered "Michelle, I will not be able to deal with this. Can
you put all the arrangements together?" I replied, "yes mom,
you can count on me to take care of everything,
as usual."

Our mother did not attend the funeral.

In Remembrance

leaves like teardrops
trickle thoughts
incomplete puzzles
cast away on water's edge

birds flee nests
hypnotized
by the sun's
crystal lyre

drunken pines mourn the loss
of what was
leafy winds dance in celebration
of what is

bristling hopes inhale
ripples of blue sky
full moon waters bow
to the task of letting go

as departed loved ones
reflect
in purled
hushed cadences

diamond memories
chime
in remembrance
of my time with you

I dream of your face
in melancholy shadows
of dewy spun
sung . . . yesterdays

How ironic that in the final moments of our lives every second seems sacred as our hearts spit out memories buried throughout the years—the laughter, the tears, the unfairness of it all.

My relationship with each sibling is unalike. Each one of us reacted to life's challenges with different tools and perceptions. Much like snowflakes, we journeyed through similar circumstances—but our reactions are our own, as we continue our separate journeys.

All That Jazz and Yoga

*Y*oga and voice share the unity of breath and body.
The power of vibration rejuvenates my cells,
fills them with light,
melts away the inner clutter of my mind
allowing me to shine from the inside out.
I visualize sound and breath melting away tense muscles
to deepen my yoga postures.
I plant my roots in the belly of my soul,
helping me create a solid foundation—a platform
under the breath that makes it possible to increase
and decrease the pressure inside my torso and facilitate
movement.
My breath is free to travel up and down my spine,
like branches of a tree.
The deeper I am rooted, the more I
can sustain strong winds.
Yoga teaches me to listen to my body—what it likes,
what it needs to liberate my voice,
leading me to a place of acceptance and stillness.

Stillness

invites songs of crickets
to beat within my heart
Stillness
invites soft winds to caress
my pale cheeks
Stillness
invites my troubled soul
to sing with gentle rains
Stillness
invites dancing lyrical
brooks to tickle my toes
Stillness
invites me to be one
with the morning sun

The enemy of my voice is the doubting-self
where all judgment, pain, sorrow, and fear live
sabotaging my unique singing gift.
When fear and disdain take control, I become nervous
drown in all the negatives,
forcing my voice to sink deep in my body,
where it manifests as tension,
and is silenced.
I must acknowledge my fears,
let go of age-old baggage locked within my mind,
trapped in energy centers along my spine.
Replace negative thoughts with positive affirmations.
My relationship with my voice seeps into all aspects of my life.
As I learn to love my voice—I learn to love me.
When I love myself first, flaws and all, unconditionally,
I will attract what I need, plant myself in love and become
my own best teacher.

Beyond my mind
is a mystical place
which holds the
key to my heart,
unleashing a
merriment of songs
riding on wings
of fireflies.

The crystal notes
listen clearly
to the symphonic
voicings of my soul,
allowing passion
joy and euphoria
as my memory gets
lost in the pain
of yesterday's
atonal melodies
of discontent.

and All that JAZZ

The hushed soul of jazz captures musical subtleties and
nuances, like a whisper
connecting vulnerability with the nakedness of me.

In the spring, trees show off their blossoms and new buds.
In the summer they are blanketed, robed in majestic leaves.
In the fall, trees dazzle with an array of colors—golds,
reds, yellows, and oranges, shining in magnificent glory.
And just when I rise and give trees a standing ovation,
they shed their leaves to reveal the bareness of their branches,
allowing me to embrace their hidden greatness.
Through winter's winds, storms, sleet, snow, and hail,
I marvel at their strength—
peaceful, strong,
enough.

Like jazz, trees teach me less is more.

Like a tree
I dig deep within,
find the sacred vulnerable space between
sound and silence,
where the heart of jazz originates.
I listen to the instruments around me,
react, question, answer
and make the song my own.

I feel jazz in an unconventional way.
Unlike classical music—which stresses the first and third beats,
making me feel grounded and secure on a familiar path—
jazz transforms me into rocky unknown territory —
stressing the second and fourth beats,
inspiring me to push aside

what I think my life should be, and fully live my life now.
There is much freedom when you are off the beat.
It allows untraditional creativity, accenting
the unexpected
preparing us to be open to it
in music as well as in life.

Jazz teaches me to turn my lessons into blessings.
There are no wrong notes in improvisation. If I land on a wrong note,
I can slide up or down a half step and will find where I belong,
be fresh in my approach, look for new things to inspire.
Never blind myself with only the melody, instead
pay attention to all components that make up a song—
the bass line and harmonic structure.
Take turns improvising with others —listen, share, and care.
By being free in my approach, I'll find what works best for me
and create something original each time because I, too, am new,
my mind free,
my surroundings and insights forever growing.

Jazz helps me eliminate anticipation—
as I allow music to unfold
and watch in awe where it guides me,
like traveling to a new country—no expectation, new language,
different culture.
There's a personal, intimate connection when I get lost in a song,
I feel the music with my whole body.
The gift of being present, centered in a peaceful place, heart
full of warmth and light, mind emptied and clear.
My voice soars when it's not judged or ridiculed. Singing
becomes a mystical journey of acceptance into my heart —a
meditation.

Music is a series of questions and answers—like a conversation,
it teaches me
to listen to what others are saying.
Both sound and silence are essential in music and in life.
We all need the yin and the yang to feel complete—
without conflict/opposition we are unbalanced.

Summer's magical transformation into autumn
reminds me change doesn't have to be scary,
but necessary
to progress to the next season.
A new reason to grow, expand, create.
I learn from nature to embrace newness.
There's beauty in every falling leaf
waiting to be transformed.
My approach to jazz is there are no wrong notes.
My approach to life is there are no mistakes, just lessons.

My heart is quilted in the
tapestry
of the early morning pastel sky
My heart echoes
the notes
of birds celebrating a new day

My heart sheds a tear
each time I doubt
my unique mastery

My heart releases
gratitude as my voice and soul
reach for the stars

I yearn to be something more
my heart believes
I am enough

A Cappella Fly Away

Fly away, little sparrow, fly away
from sins of traditions past.
Set yourself free of yesteryears' storms.
Find a fresh voice, a new beginning.
Flee, tainted songs of your ancestors
in search of untouched melodies.
For unto us, let your voice be heard,
innocent and void
of past transgressions.
Transformed by the light
from whence you came,
in search of a home,
you can call your own.
Fly away, little sparrow, fly away.

Since my parents' divorce when I was twelve,
holidays were a tug of war—
who goes with whom.
My mother lived in Concord, my dad in Marlboro.
Both parents drowning in booze,
scraping their pockets to provide a bit of normalcy,
spewing sharp cutting words
at the dinner table
until collapsed drunk on the sofa.

In high school and college, I was
blessed
to find friends who opened
their homes to me,
but I still felt like a feral cat —
trying to scratch a way in,
longing for a forever dwelling.

The holidays are here
the Ebenezer in me
lurks in the dark
bringing presents
of loneliness and guilt
tied with ribbons of pain.
Was it something
I said or did
under the mistletoe?
The black coal
of my cut ancestor ties
fills my stocking
as I watch
Hallmark card
family traditions
yearning and alone.

At age 20, I began a major quest in search
of my own clan and by age 23,
I met a smart, idealistic young man
who was working on his doctorate, loved to cook,
and made me laugh.
Together we started a new life,
undefined by my past.
A life I hoped, would help me establish a home.
A life where no one drank or popped pills.

In Israel an Orthodox conversion is never refuted.
My new family wanted
to make sure our children would be Jewish.
So, I studied the laws of Judaism for a year before my
wedding.
Knowing when I converted,
the children I would have and I,
would be embraced wherever I went, no matter what country
or state.
I would have a place where I belonged,
and be welcomed into the households and hearts of a
community.
Every week I congregated
in the synagogue
joined in a feast with friends and loved ones
on Friday night, Saturday lunch,
and the meal before it all ends at sunset
called a "shala shudis" (third feast).
Imagine every week a holiday like
Christmas and Thanksgiving.
There's a blessing—*bracha* for every instant of life,
leaving nothing in your soul temple
to be taken for granted.

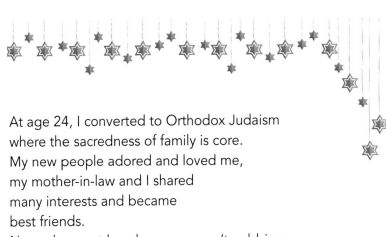

At age 24, I converted to Orthodox Judaism
where the sacredness of family is core.
My new people adored and loved me,
my mother-in-law and I shared
many interests and became
best friends.
Not a day went by when we weren't gabbing
on the phone for hours.
Mother Di, my High School music teacher
was my matron of honor and
walked me down the aisle with her husband Joe.
I wanted my wedding to be perfect,
no worries, so
I didn't invite my relatives.
I erased them from my life,
along with performing
on Fridays and Saturdays, a major sacrifice.
But I gained the life
I always dreamt of.

Adagio-Shabbat

Dancing neon flames
integrate wordless songs
to our souls.

Phantom shadows sing the smells
of golden Shabbat challah
sweetened with tears and harmony.

Scarlet wine seals our devotion
as we give thanks for a day of rest
uniting our community,

while we stop and listen
to the sounds of silence.
Our voices join

to celebrate the inner light
of our blessings.
Now and forever.... Amen

One of the complications while searching for a family is taking on the personality (melody) of the *new* family. You act like a chameleon and take on the identity of others and sometimes lose yourself in the process. It's funny, those who know me think I am a unique individual; a free bird unable to be caged. People can't believe that I would ever give up *performing* in exchange for a family. Never mind erasing my past to convert to Orthodox Judaism where I embraced a new life and was part of an even bigger family—a community.

Drinking the stillness
of the night
while the moon
drifts in sleep
I am awakened
by a lark
peering in the dark
to outstretched stars.

Lurking in the vastness
a young girl
hypnotized by singing
tree shadows

unable to hear
the celestial melody
kept secret
yearns to be

included
in the symphonic game
but is unable
to join in the evening song.

Classical Technique
Caught up in the Technicalities

The Laws

*J*udaism teaches to seize God's world with a spirit of gratitude. Blessings remind us to approach the world with appreciation and it is recommended we say one hundred blessings a day. Leaving nothing to be taken for granted.

As a sincere convert who tried to succeed in this new world, I embraced the many laws. Rabbis believed my soul was resurrected from a Jewish seed planted from the beginning of time. I was surrounded by intellectual, sober individuals who put family first.
We are the company we keep.

Kashrut (kosher)

Bound by laws and foreign recipes
from ancient traditions,
my table a sacred temple
simmers the laws of kashrut.

Meat and dairy cannot be stewed together,
as it says in the Torah:
do not boil a kid in its mother's milk (Exodus 23:19)
I can only digest—
land animals with cloven (split) hooves
that chew the cud, meaning they must eat grass so—
no pork.
Seafood must have fins and scales,
no shellfish or bottom feeders.
I will miss eating lobster, shrimp, and crab.

Meat and dairy dishes, pans, silverware and sponges
are stocked in separate parts of my kitchen.
We are what we eat
and if we must eat meat
let us kill an animal causing no pain.

Slaughter is performed by a specially
trained person known as a "Shochet"
his long, razor-sharp knife known as a "chalef"
renders the animal insensible to pain with a single cut.

There is a marinating of time
before we can eat dairy after consuming meat.
My husband insists we follow a European heritage custom
and wait six hours which frustrates me, as most of our
friends wait three hours.

There are no kosher restaurants in DC,
I create many gourmet
recipes right in my own kitchen.
Cooking has always braised a positive place in my young heart—
by my dad's side
as I watched the love he kneaded in his culinary creations.

Recipes of love

Dad,
I try to remember the cadence of a song
or
the sparkle in your eyes
as you beat eggs for a cake.

The mixture stirs up
memories
of young me
assisting by your side.

As I watch with awe and
wonderment
peaks of frosting spiraled
a glimmering spectacle.

Licking the beaters
icing
dancing down our chins
our hearts dissolved.

Aromas sang
to our senses
as we removed its' golden essence
gently from the oven.

Was it a special occasion
like
my birthday or a holiday?
My memory fades.

All I recall is
cherishing
the ingredients in your
smile.

Shabbat —The Sabbath

The Sabbath refuels my soul,
time to read, sing shabbat chants
at the table and synagogue,
relax and stop the world.
No work can be done after I light candles
and recite the blessing,
embracing the entrance of Shabbat
bringing rest to my heart and home.
Lights on timers,
as hot plates keep prepared food warm,
I enjoy the break from the fast pace of the week,
give thanks and say a prayer
over kiddush wine —the fruits of our labors
and honey challah splashed with the salt of our ancestors' tears
and the sweetness of tomorrow.

The numerous holidays
keep me in a cooking frenzy
which I love.
Many new friends walk miles
for my homemade delicacies,
since there is no driving on the Sabbath and holidays.
The community embraces me like family
and I feel, for once,
that I truly belong.

Life's Bounty

Come let us drink
the notes
of sweet wine
giving life
to the wondrous
heartbeat
resounding in our soul

The poetry
of our lives
nestles
in the lyrics
of our favorite songs
flowered in vines
of our existence

We sip the winds
of rain
drunk in the choruses
of a new
tomorrow
We uncork
the undying
powers
of the fruits of a new song

The laws of shabbat and keeping kosher are not difficult for
me.
But the other laws are a challenge which I rationalize in hopes
of acceptance.

Tzniut—Modesty

A married woman must cover her hair
all females should wear clothes that are modest—
nothing skintight and it is required
to cover knees, elbows, and collarbone.

Niddah—Menstrual Impurity

As a touchy-feely French woman, the laws of niddah numb
my heart.
They were initially based in the Torah. Leviticus 15:19 states,
*"When a woman has a discharge, her discharge being blood
from her body, she shall remain in her impurity for seven days;
whoever touches her shall be unclean."*

All public displays of affection
between husband and wife are inappropriate.
In private, when a woman has her menses
there can be no sexual activity.
She and her husband must sleep in separate beds
and not touch or pass objects to one another—
like the salt shaker,
which might lead to further touching.

After all discharge is ended
a woman is required to wait
seven clean days before
she goes to purify herself in a kosher mikveh,
and only then,
her husband is obligated to
resume intimate relations with her.

Mikveh—Ritual Bath

Naked I stand in hopes of rebirth.
A *yidisha* mama
hair scarfed in commitment,
her many religious children
perhaps eight or ten line her face
with pride and exhaustion.
She searches my naked body for vanity—
no jewelry, no makeup,
nails cut short
void of polish,
no beauty products on hair or skin.
After fourteen days of no physical
contact with my husband
her touch tickles with speculation
as she makes sure
there are no stray hairs on my body
from my long-combed hair,
vaginal and armpit areas
before I submerge in prayer
under water.
My skin and hair immersed
in this well of purification—a mikveh.
Soaked in disbelief,
I pray the waters drown
my shame of loneliness and allow
the notes of my soul
to join in song
as they ripple through water
and shimmer with the stars.

Let the winds of yesterday blow
into the winds of tomorrow,
leaving the heart of today
to bask in tomorrow's glory.

Since my husband's family wasn't Orthodox, I assumed we would lighten up on some of these archaic laws and just keep kosher, observe the sabbath and holidays. Sometimes we must reject what we think our life should be, to live the life, we're in. But along with the process of my conversion, my husband became a *born-again* religious Jew, embracing all the laws to the letter. It did earn us the respect and trust of the Chassidic/Orthodox community.

I tried to stay positive and convince myself
that the laws of niddah would help us
work on the attentiveness
part of our relationship every month
while abstaining from physical contact.
Passion cannot last forever,
friendship can.
So, each month I waited for the mikveh waters
to bring me healing energy.

My body dormant
like the cocoon
of a butterfly
awaits to drink
peaceful wines
of my soul,
emptying pain
of yesteryears.
I begin to nest,
my pregnant mind
adjusts to the realities
of my new existence
erupting
herculean, blazing flashes
of my washed-out youth,
as I prepare to give birth
to my future omniscient self
flowering my one true voice.

Kol Isha— A Woman's Voice

The singing voice of a woman
is considered sensual
and possibly stimulating to males.
It is therefore forbidden for a man
to hear a woman other than his immediate family sing,
and men are prohibited to pray
or study Torah in that environment.

The modern-orthodox Jewish community, of which we were members, did not really obey these laws, as they were for extremists.
And my voice was so needed and loved by the community.

Little did I know...

Cantatas Little did I know

Little did I know,
life's detours
would navigate me
into flood waters
of new opportunities.

Little did I know,
barriers limiting
performing
would lead
to my teaching voice.

Little did I know,
teaching would fill the void
created by restrictions
from my new orthodox life
and cast me
in adventures of creativity.

Little did I know,
I had a gift for directing
folks of all ages
to find their own unique talents.

Little did I know
some things are meant to be
as major changes
forced me to dig and explore
many unknown possibilities.

Little did I know,
the divine fruits of my life
were blanketed
in nature's inspired
symphonies

leading me down a path
of triumphant glory.

I always believed everything in life happens for a reason.
The bigger the challenges—
the more power to grow, understand and evolve.

I am not broken.
I must remember, true art
is chiseled from all the fractured pieces of life.
Let the sharp edges define me,
rather than cut through me.
Let the smooth one's shimmer with the sun,
both are necessary to succeed.
I am my own masterpiece.
The voicings of my soul are the nucleus
of each note I sing.

As a director, I could always spot actors who had experienced much pain and hardship. The personal baggage they brought to their role encouraged depth and vulnerability to their character. They were able to feel and express a broader range of emotions.

Performing and directing for me, has been an outlet to
unscramble my mind of emotions I needed to set free.
Working through my characters' desires and flaws helped me
understand my own. And because of this, I was able to share
these insights with my performers and the results made for
powerful productions.

As a teacher, I learned from the many instructors of my life.
There are different levels of educators just like there are
different levels of musicians.

There are musicians who tinker with their instruments
and make excuses
for not progressing.
They are like incompetent teachers who blame
students for not growing or learning.

There are musicians who practice every day
five to eight hours
because it does not come easy.
They are book smart and can copy other performers
but lack their own voice and creativity.
They are like teachers who follow lesson plans,
are very organized and go by the book.

Then, there are musicians who are born brilliant.
It comes naturally to them.
They wear their music
like a worn in, favorite pair of jeans.
Music blossoms from their souls.
So too, are gifted teachers
who think outside the box,
inspire, care
and share their knowledge.
They never give up on students
who give up on themselves,

but rather teach them
to celebrate the journey and struggle
of learning something new.
They bring a totally new level of instruction.
And those are the teachers
who find their way into our hearts and stay forever.
Their commitment and passion are infectious
transforming
not only their students but
future generations.

Little did I know,
by the age of fifty-five
I would accomplish more than I ever imagined.
I would go on to instruct in over thirty schools.
I would own three performing arts centers,
start numerous theater companies,
direct hundreds of shows,
perform in musicals, cabarets, jazz clubs,
and big bands across the east coast.
And teach thousands of students,
all of whom I carry in my heart,
including some
who have achieved stardom
in the performing arts world.

Little did I know,
magic happens
when I let go
of the grip
of expectation.

Ode To a Gifted Teacher

The butterfly drifts in a
kaleidoscope of dreams.
Stirring our imagination
with songs of eternal summer.
Imprinting life's lessons
from flower to flower.
Its delicate wonderment
propels us to look to the sun
and give thanks to all that must
be cherished and loved.
As it flutters off into the sunset
birds begin to sing
their evening songs and
we are transformed.

Chords Motherhood

A Miracle Within

*B*illowy breasts suspend
over a mountainous womb,
swollen feet
carry me awkwardly
across new waters.

I feel your touch,
giggle as you hiccup.
My legs wobble in disbelief.
Yesterday I ran with the wind,
today I struggle against the tides.

Your kicks grow stronger.
I am in awe
of your fingers
plucking the strings of my heart.
Maybe snowflakes
sprinkled you inside me,
or raindrops
watered your secret
garden within me.

I celebrate
the miracle of you.
Feed your body hope,
nourishment from seeds
of spring,
perfumed flowers of summer,
rustling multi-colored leaves of fall,
the blizzard mightiness of winter.

I breathe into your veins
all-encompassing songs
of your ancestors
as we become one with Nature
and all who have stood before us,
the crystal heart beating inside you
so delicate, so fragile
… so strong

In Preparation

As I lie, dormant
in the tundra of yesterday
I yearn for blossoms of spring,
heat of summer,
changes fall brings.

I journey into a magical forest
in preparation
I build your nest of expectation,
wait for your arrival
with giddy anticipation.

My mind sets sail
to our first glance,
tear droplets drift
down my cheeks
Am I enough?

Can you hear my heart song,
my laughter, my cry?
Does my voice
reach out and cradle your sigh?
I long to caress
the outline of your chin,
marvel at your tiny fingers.

Oh, how I yearn to be
all you need me to be.

Help me understand patience.
Help me nurture
your unique beautiful soul,
so, you can grow

a garden full of love
compassion, understanding
soaring on rays of sunshine
and the promise of spring.

Labor Lockdown

Confined in a sterile hospital room,
clothed in a worn gray gown,
wires
wrapped around my swollen tummy.
I look down
unable to see my clown-like feet.
My stomach a volcano
ready to erupt,
my protruded bellybutton
lost in an overstretched canvas.

The day I dreamt of—
finally, here
three weeks overdue,
and thirty-six hours
since my membranes ruptured.

Left alone—
deserted by my doctor
who is in another town and hospital
on-call for a friend
on vacation.

                        I feel
                       trapped
                    in a deluge
                    of darkness
                               tears
                    like falling leaves,
                     gasp for breath
                          I suffocate
                   in my lack of control.
                    I try to hold on
                      to the beauty

of what was.
The emptiness
of winter
storms across my mind,
snowbanks
avalanche
in a blizzard
of powerless contractions.
I wait
and ponder
my demise.

Nurses pop in every hour
with apologetic, worried looks.
Time stops.
Hours a never-ending song.
I snap at my husband who checks in on me,
"How can I give birth without my music?
I want our baby brought into this world to the sounds
of Mozart, Puccini, and Debussy."
My hormones turn
into a tsunami frenzy.

The Doctor arrives at 1:30am
tired,
having just finished a difficult delivery.
Relieved,
I forget about lost days
waiting to give birth.
He gives me an internal exam.
The baby is in distress,
must perform an emergency C-Section.

As they wheel me to the operating room
my head spins.
How could my baby be stressed?

I was attentive to everything my doctor said—
gave up weightlifting, walked & swam every day,
drank herbal teas,
ate only healthy foods.

Fear wears at the senses
masking
perpetual melodies
of triumphant morning birds,
the beauty of today devoured
by the bitterness
of yesterday.

Fear wears at the senses
masking
sincere words spoken
disabling music once celebrated,
incapable to find
peace of mind
as dreams turn into screams.

Fear envelops my heart,
my eyes swell in tears
I try to stay positive
praying
to the universe to look down on me
and grant me this one and only wish—a healthy baby.

Delivery

Smells of alcohol permeate the room
my husband clenches my hand,
his eyes mask terror
with a faint smile,
as he watches them cut me open.
In a matter of seconds,
a piercing cry echoes,
the announcement *it's a girl!*
I burst in relief
and ask if she is alright,
the nurse smiles.
"She has all her fingers and toes and looks healthy."
They rush her to isolation before I can hold her,
where they keep her under watch for twenty-four hours.

Sara Rebecca born at 2:47am on December 17, 1984,
named after her two deceased great grandmothers,
a Jewish custom
to keep their loving memory alive.

Elated, my husband and I
call and wake up his parents,
her Bubbie and Zadie to announce the news.
Bubbie is thrilled–a girl.
Having only sons, she couldn't wait to hit the stores
and buy frilly dresses.

It is the first day of Hanukah,
and twelve hours to shabbat
which in Orthodox practical terms means—
no phone, driving or electrical tampering.
My husband will leave soon
to spend Shabbat at home and in the synagogue.

I lay in my private hospital room
alone,
aware of the stitches stapled to my lower abdomen
and discomfort from the whole ordeal.
The nurses bring me food,
check how my breast pumping is going,
and give me an update on my baby.
They bring a picture of my little girl
trying to scream
her way out of isolation.
"She hasn't stopped crying since the second she was
brought to ICU—
good luck and rest up. You are going to need it."
I glare,
"She just misses her mother's voice.
It isn't her fault she was put *on hold*
until the doctor got his ass in the delivery room."
This is the longest, day I have ever experienced.

Finally, after twenty-four grueling hours,
my baby is brought to me.
I hold her in my arms,
so delicate at 6 pounds 14 ounces,
her heart-shaped face outlines
shiny intense eyes,
her turned-up button nose,
and rosy cheeks.
My heart soars.

So That's What You Look Like My Precious Child

Lost in a tunnel maze
of iris blurred mosaic branches
your mouth latches
wet sweetness releases
squirts you in the eyes
to my surprise
hoses splash
I clasp to restrain
overflowing waters
now calm
blanketed
in the warmth
of your newborn silkiness
I massage your little foot
eyes locked
to the beat
of your gulp
as you fall asleep in my arms

So That's What You Look Like Mama

your songs
have serenaded
me to sleep
for all my eternity
your whispers
like babbling brooks
have soothed my soul
your cries
have echoed
on wings of butterflies

the beat
of your heart
kept me calm
through many a storm
and sleepless night
I see
the moon in your eyes
a river in your smile
your laugh
a gentle breeze
on a hot summer day

for months
I have tossed
and turned
yearning
to feel your touch
now a beam of light
shines on you
as you hold me
in your arms

you are my sun
my moon
my everything
my mama

Content and at peace.
I have a daughter —Sara
which means princess in Hebrew.
    I promise to be the mother I never had.

The Prince of Ishah

Once upon a time, many lullabies later,
there lived a Queen
whose heart was nestled
on a mountaintop overlooking carpets
of evergreens and coral granite castles.
Guarded by all the birds of the forest,
she sat in exuberant anticipation
of the birth of her second child.

The stork flew by announcing it was time,
the Queen let out a musical note which reached the high
heavens,
as a son was born to her.
He immediately latched onto her breast
and the animal kingdom
let out a melodious howl of delight.
All was peaceful and this little prince
with fiery sunrise hair and eyes rooted
deep in the earth's crust
was named by his sister, Princess Sara—
Zachary,
which in the ancient language
means *"remembered by God."*

As he got older, he began to explore
with his sister
the mountains and waterfalls of Lake Como,
in search of lost salamanders and other orphan critters.
The prince's language was one of the forest—*Ishah*
and he taught his many friends
the secret tongue
of how to listen with your heart.
　　　No mother was prouder.

Dissonance Warts of My Demise

Infected with doubt
past sins
from family ties
disguised as warts
bubble under my nails,
cracking cuticles.
Afraid to transfer
to my kids,
I burn away
black rooted
sizzling flesh
releasing
smells of guilt.
Needle in hand,
I pick away
oozing skin
hoping to forget
throbbing horror
of a life without love.
My head dizzy with pain
sleeps
in a bucket of numbness so,
I may protect
my children from the
warts of my demise.

I'm an actor. I can play all the parts: mother, daughter, wife, sister, lover, chef, housekeeper, entertainer, teacher. I have done it for many years. I keep my life together filling the voids of an empty heart. But sometimes, I have no control over the way my body reacts to hidden emotions and fears.
I worried much of my life about passing my mother's mental illness on to my kids.

My Addiction

Teaching became my drug,
an escape
from the emptiness
of a loveless marriage.
My dopamine pathway
to motivation, pleasure,
and rewards.
The high of watching a student conquer
their mind's limitations
became an obsession.
My children participated
in awe.
I was fixed on
directing plays, musicals,
and cabaret performances.
When one was completed
the withdrawal
left me feeling
empty
until the next project
fed my compulsion
to new heights
and accomplishments.
I felt invincible
living on adrenaline—
not sleep.
I was hooked
and in five years
achieved
more than I ever expected
in my lifetime.
The admiration of my children
only adding to my high.

Finale

I always believed the sun
would forever shine on us.
Darkness
would turn into
the eternal promise
of a new day
with you,
by my side.
I never expected bitter
winds to spiral us
in different directions.
Lost
from one another
conversation
silenced,
ambivalence more spiteful
than any unkept secret.
I wait
patiently for the stars
to reappear
on many a stormy night,
rains to subside and release
the pain
of a marriage
bonded in hopes and dreams.
Now washed away
by separate streams
numb
broken remnants
of a sacred union
tossed out with the trash.
I always believed
our relationship would last.

Who Am I

Disjointed notes of a song,
lost without harmony.
Scattered, jumbled
pieces of refrains
unable to fit and connect.
Sound stops
drowns in oblivion.

I sit
choked with tears,
eyes moist.
I attempt to escape
in a bluesy ballad,
sultry weighted lyrics
stray
in a walking bassline
seizing the decay
of many unanswered questions.
I struggle to find a familiar tune
instead of a blank melody.

I erased myself from my family on French Hill
to find a new wholesome family and now I can't find me.
I need to connect with the me before I converted to Judaism.
My voice is drowning, and I don't know how to save it.

There's an emptiness
I can't seem to fill.
Am I crazy like my mother?
I lie awake
yearning to drown in a blanket of dreams
where the rhythmic beating of my heart
silences my guilt-fed mind.
I lie awake,
eyes locked open,
trying to let go of the nonstop melody
of my consciousness.
I lie awake,
never to fall into deep, peaceful slumber.

At that point in my life, I didn't have the answers.
Answers would come years later.

Modulation Change

Modulation in music;
 a change from one tonality to another,
 used to add interest,
 trigger varying emotions
 and expand the heart of the listener.

 I wonder if I can view my life as a series of modulations?

Here I am, in my forties, lost in a pool of second guesses.
My kids despise me for walking away from their Jewish
upbringing and turning their identities upside down.

My dreams lead
me down a corridor
of shame
where guilt tortures
and unravels
many who are close to me.

The constant lashing
of my words
torment and scar,
trickling regret
as I try to forgive
and forget.

Tables turn
sacrifices are made
like a lamb grazing
before the slaughter.
Who is right?
Who is wrong?
Why must this game change
interrupt my song?

Eyes once cherished
now, filled with despair
singing of injustice
when I was unaware.

Tables turn,
the story unfolds
and we are lost at sea.

Our minds resurrect baggage
from past ironies,
when hearts were young
protected by armored innocence.

But now, age has branded us,
our lives tattered with doubt
and unanswered questions.

Who is right?
Who is wrong?
The apathy lives on
and so does my song.

Lost Lullabies

From the time of your birth
you always had a song in your heart.
Like a bird at dawn,
you felt *part of this world*,
and had a *Secret Garden*
of books you would read
until your eyes sunk,
book clutched to your chest.

Now in your teens,
your room looks like Dante's *Inferno*,
painted murals on ceiling and walls
of angel's eyes dark in despair
crying blood,
scarred pain and anger
  knitted on arms and legs,
crucified palms
pleading for help,
desperate to be set free.

I stand powerless,
searching for lullabies
to soothe and calm.

I watch my daughter dissolve
in a pool of bitterness
as she tries
to be the perfect body image
of her imprisoned mind.
She reminds me of all my past sins
as a mother.
Times I may have broken
her spirit with impatience,

or didn't listen—
always needing to give advice.
Our strong personalities pounding
each other to the ground.
I, wanting desperately to be liked by her,
forgot she needed me
to be a mother
not a friend.

Imperfect Melodies

I remember when you were young,
my son,
branched to my hip
melodically sucking your thumb
your gaze rooted to my heart

United we traveled
I, your Queen
you, my little prince
eyes crooning
as you softly caressed my cheek

Just three years of age
baseball cap off to the side
seems like yesterday
bathed in a dream
splashed with laughter

In adolescence you watched me
search for lost puzzle pieces
of my existence
our worlds scrambled
and though my heart wanted more

I never forgot the melancholy notes
in your eyes
as I drowned
in a torch song
of limitations

Never again would you smile
at me with trust,
your heart now vaulted
protective of
all who have hurt you

You modulated
near and far
searching for answers
escaping broken melodies
of your bitter divorced childhood

And I, left behind
with severed pieces
of my imperfections
yearning to
cradle you

in my arms,
serenade you
forever
with songs of love
and understanding

my sweet
delicate prince
with strawberry
blond hair
and sand castle eyes

Stormy Weather

Lost in the confines of my bed
blankets cradle
stormy thoughts.
Branches bend, jump
snap in a gasp
on newly thawed guilt
of what was,
what could have been.
Winds of thunder
stomp my rooftop
turning my life inside out.
Through forest trees
I flee with leaves
in a frenzy
in search of who I once was,
down dirt path hills
piling in mounds
of soon to be blossoms.
Birds drift in and out
of harm's way
and I, paralyzed
bruised in fear
from past mistakes
beg for guidance.
I yearn for the maternal sun
to warm my aching heart.
Clouds mourn,
hold the dark
refuse to move on.
Winds continue to upset regret
and peaceful law and order
with iced squall tantrums

destroying buds of today
from the babes of yesterday.

My mother got divorced after twelve years of marriage.
I always told myself I would never repeat her mistakes—I lasted
sixteen years.

I failed my family.
I failed myself.

Marilyn's Song for my Mother-in-Law

I miss
riding down roadways
of many lost conversations
chatted daily,
tears of laughter
sharing recipes of our lives
singing the ends
of our favorite songs.

I miss
our mother-daughter
musical revival,
you the red, red robin
always bob, bob, bobbin
I forever wanting *much more.*

You held my hand
through sleepless nights.
I cherished
the many miles
we rode together.

Now you are gone
separated from me.
I attempt to modulate
alone
down the road chiseled
by your love,
compassion
and heart songs.

What I Saw

I visited my mother today
after decades of forgotten,
lost melodies.
Her body decaying
scratching for life
with eyes of steel.

No doubt, terrified of the bed
she had made.
Drunk and consumed
by what she despised.
Her stare seemed to yell
of guilt
as her armored heart
once again,
shielded her.
Frozen
sculpted sloppily in a chair
sucking oxygen
from her TV remote,
afraid to change
the channels
of her existence.
I watched
forever
damaged
in numbness.

It's Time to Forgive.

Running away from my childhood,
I spiraled full circle,
spinning around cracked rings of my maternal tree.
The cross-section of my existence
leads to the concentric patterns of our lives,
causing me to reflect—

My mother loved her dad and despised her mom.
My daughter loves her dad and despises me.
My mother converted to Catholicism in her late teens
and became a nun before meeting my father.
I converted to Judaism in my early twenties after I met my
husband to be.
My mother got divorced after twelve years of marriage,
I, after sixteen years.
My mother escaped life through alcohol and sex,
I, with music and theater.
My mother married a man who loved to cook
as did I.
My mother and I were separated in high school and lived apart.
My daughter and I were separated when she was in high
school.

Anger and resentment are internal wastelands.
It is time to modulate
to forgiveness
so, I can open myself to clues
about the conditions and magnitude of emotions
I attached to in my formative years.
Time for me to take a step back
look into my own trunk
of love, heartache, and growth.
I can't change yesterday, but I can create a new today.

I release the pain of my mother for not knowing how to be a better parent, always in competition, berating me, criticizing my body, and making me feel *never enough*—no matter what I accomplished.
I forgive my mother for not loving me. How could she, when she didn't love herself?

I close my eyes,
swim in these cramped feelings.
I exhale affliction,
gasping for salvation.

I am saved by the strong,
innocent child within.
She holds me tight.
I cradle her beautiful,
unique, warrior soul.

My tears drown in the suffocated
breath of my numb heart.
I ride the waves of these submerged,
locked feelings.

gray
ice blotched
        memories
            wash
                down
            water banks
                cleansing
                the bitterness
                        of yesterday's
                            sun rays
    accompany
            songs
        of docile
    birds
        singing
in the glory
    of a new
        dawn
            tree
                roots
                bathe
        in the promise
            of spring
            I thank
            the universe
        for another
    blessed morning

Life isn't about deleting the past to enter the present.
I must understand and learn from it first,
like a modulation—
how can it expand my heart and help me grow?

On my deck railing
a little chickadee was perched,
eyes clenched shut.
Is this a sign
like the one given to me when I was eleven,
right before my parents' divorce?
I gently took the tiny bird in my hands.
Tears escalated,
my heart discharged all angst
as the bird opened its eyes
and seemed to say:

> *Do not allow life*
> *to harden your heart*
> *with pain and sorrow.*

I released it in the air
along with my remorse.
This time I'm not starting
from scratch,
I come with well-earned lessons,
learned from many mistakes,
and life experiences.

I will soften my heart
with the promise of many tomorrows.
I am ready
to view the modulations
in my life
as a positive force,
vital to my growth.

Harmony Healing

Spring Awakens

*J*ust as winter melts
to make room for spring
so do tears flow
to help us grow new wings.

Just as insecurity
is rooted in overcompensation
harmony bathes
in stillness celebration.

Just as nature thrives
in the slow rhythm of promise
we too, can plant and nurture
our own garden of calmness.

Learning to love myself, was the beginning of my healing process journey—a major contradiction to my religious faith growing up, where I was taught to put others first.
Learning to say *no* to people was a challenge—it took a lot of practice to rid myself of the guilt. Do something because you want to —not because you worry people won't like you.
My time spent with loved ones is now about quality, filled with awareness and joy.

Feeling defective and unworthy drowned my ability to accept myself for who I truly am.
I stopped running away from my past and embraced it as part of my journey —pain and all. I now understand, other people's limitations are not my own.
I now love myself, flaws, and all.
And just because I can give 100 percent, I shouldn't expect it from others.

Letting go of resentment and hurt, opened the door to my inner wisdom. I'm not perfect. I've made mistakes, some life-changing, leading me down a stray path. But sometimes we must lose what is dear, to realize how necessary it is in our life.

A receptive heart nurtures my inner child, who is goodness and love, untouched by the frightening world. I continue to follow the path to my heart, it helps me explore the hearts of others, no matter how difficult it might be at times.

The most important lesson I have learned is that we are all born with a teacher and a student within.
Sometimes we're the teacher, sometimes the student. As we grow, honor, and acknowledge this duality within us, we become wiser, more content.

I've encountered many teachers through the years.
Some were blessings and some—lessons.
The ones who were blessings
helped me grow
and nurture my teacher within by believing in me.

They will forever be stamped in my heart.

I now realize that I was able to attract what I needed
to survive growing up in my life
and had a few substitute-mothers
to guide me…
and I had nature and music.

I proudly wear the scars
of the people who were my lessons.
The pain, fear, and heartache I endured
made me strong—
a survivor,
many times, forcing me to forge a new path.
I wear those scars with honor,
they remind me
of all I have survived.
Evil lurking in the shadows
of my mind,
twisted my heart and strangled
the beauty of what was once pure.
I watched as laughter
quickly turned to tears
and how fast I could become
what I despised.
My dreams held prisoner as my fears were infected
with bitterness and despair,
until one day I awoke unknown to myself,
not knowing how or why, I traveled so far.

Fortunately, the heart and soul of my inadequate childhood
home was fueled by music. It helped me escape the torment
of many troubled times.

Music doesn't judge pain. It sympathizes and frees it. So, if you want to understand my affliction, listen to Samuel Barber's *Adagio for Strings* or the music from the movies *Schindler's List* or *Cinema Paradiso*. There's beauty in pain, that can only be expressed through music.

Music taught me the meaning of happy tears—why is it when my heart smiles, tears sound down my cheek.

Thank you, Mom, for bringing me into this beautiful, symphonic world where I can begin and end each day with a song. Thank you, Dad, for teaching me the importance of good food, laughter, and music at the dining room table.

So here I am, full circle—
teacher, student, mother, partner, friend.
Now it is I, who sits back in awe
as I watch seeds planted
so many years ago
grow and bloom.
The blossoms of my voice
shimmer
through the evening skies
awakening hearts
longing to be set free.
I reflect in astonishment
how much I've learned
from the unrestricted boundaries
of my own unique self.
I am now one
with my teacher and student
as I journey into the heart.
My voice, a gift to share with this world.

Today, I retire my battered sword and surrender to the present moment.

Tiny whisperings beat strongly as I give birth to my *wise self*. *My wise self*, who always believed I was pure in heart.

My wise self, who stood by me all my life, watching me grow and stumble like a toddler as I overachieved, conquered, and danced the frenzy of life's accomplishments—living every moment to its fullest but never taking time to rest and celebrate the divine within.

My wise self, patiently awaited me, with glimpses of infinity in the stars, stillness of the earth, and songs of the wind that encircled my mind as I would practice music, tai-chi, Reiki, meditation, and yoga. It's been a long pregnancy and an even longer delivery. But after a life of exploring all the possibilities, my greatest accomplishment is giving birth
to *my one true self*,
who I remember at age five
with her cute button nose and pixie hair,
singing and wishing upon the stars.

Once I was fueled by anxiety.
Now I'm fueled by awareness.

As the sun melts away
the morning frost
from my branches

Mirroring the day's
endless
possibilities

I reach for birds' wings
hoping
to be serenaded

The innocence of my youth
tucked away under
my sculpted bark

I peer down
at billowy
majestic mountains

A servant to nature
feeling small
knowing I am rooted

To the symphonic
glory
surrounding me

The stormy hardships
of just yesterday
disappear in clouds

I gaze at my reflection
so mighty in the lake
blanketing my roots

I am bigger
than life
stronger than any storm

My songs caressed
by golden rays
of sunshine

As birds
sing out to me
we are all family

I will pursue my dreams
but never forget the road
that leads me home

Outro Final Notes

*S*easons change
with the wind and sun.
Trees stand strong
bending with the breeze.
Birds remain constant
starting and ending
each day in song,
never giving up
on life's erratic antidotes.

Sometimes we take their songs
for granted
as we meld
into the hustle-bustle
concerto of life.
But birds, like the leaves
of a tree
find comfort in silence.

Making sure to stand still,
to observe daily symphonies.
Their love is the voice
under all quietude,
invoking peace and kindness.
Carrying us back home,
creating eternal music
of a life well lived
a kaleidoscope of memories
written in our hearts . . . forever.

I purchased a cabin in the woods, in my forties after my
divorce, with the sole purpose of healing and creating new
memories for me and my kids.

The sounds of the creek
comforted me many sleepless nights.
Buzzing bees and wands of neons
cast a spell of iridescent stillness
on my koi pond,
inspiring thoughts to float
on lily pads.

Evenings were spent
mesmerized
by the moon,
adrift in a peaceful bliss
as starry brisk springs
awakened my youthful heart.
I bathed in the glow
of crystal water sonatas.

My rustic country home
inspired by the paintings
of Thomas Kincaid
was perfect for parties
and family gatherings.
It placed a bandage
on everyday trials and tribulations
to all who wandered
down its stone driveway,
willing to leave behind
cellular or internet reception,
transcending life
to a simpler, tranquil flow
where puzzles are built,
books read,

```
                games played
          and marshmallows roasted.
              A magical escape,
            where time stopped so,
         one could connect with nature.
```

My children were enchanted when they visited.
We shared a new life together, creating many cherished
memories.

On my fiftieth birthday, I hiked through the Canadian Rockies.
At the top of one of the wildflower mountains,
I peered out at the majestic beauty of Lake Louise
awestruck,
I collapsed on a bench,
humbled by the glacier-fed turquoise water,
rippling melodies of nostalgic lost memories,
burned down my cheeks.

A beautiful bird,
landed next to me.
I took a nut from my pocket
and shared my gratitude
with this magnificent creature—
a *Clarks Nutcracker*.
It perched on my index finger.
I continued to feed it,

content,
reinforcing
the balance of nature
so needed in my life.
No matter what the past
had brought my way
pain and rejection
did not define me.
I am enough
and just as sacred,
as this creature.

Throughout my life I have grown to understand the healing
powers of music and nature.

Life, like music, has many tempos.
We can approach it slowly, accentuate
like a swing tune, or we can rush
through accelerando style.
Life, like classical music, needs structure
and boundaries.
Life, like musical theater teaches us to burst
out in song when words fail us.
Life, like a ballad, can be full of pain and
beauty and, through pain, we can grow
and understand its' lessons. The slow
movement of a song allows us to be in
the now, celebrating every note.
Life, like a bluesy torch song, can help us
embrace the struggle and trust in the
light at the end of the tunnel.
Life, like a jazz tune, encourages us to think
outside the box while creating
our own destiny.
Life, like a Latin beat taps into the rhythm
of the heart.
Or maybe, when nothing goes as expected, we
can all learn to *scat* to home base or
rock out!

Wherever I roam I'm not alone,
the music of my life
creeps up
and is ever present.
When I take my daily walk,
I connect and remember
my first sacred experience
with music and nature,

all orchestrated to Claude Debussy's *Afternoon of a Faun*.
The Sounds of Silence by Paul Simon and Art Garfunkel
spoke to my loneliness and shame in my elementary years.
I will never forget the *Unforgettable* sound of my dad
singing with Nat King Cole's velvety voice,
or the agony of *The Man Who Got Away*,
one of my mother's favorites,
a torch song only Judy Garland, could deliver.

For many years, life was a musical
as I burst out in song when I couldn't express myself.
Yes, I was *A Cockeyed Optimist*
and *So in Love* with *The Sound of Music*.

I was such a *Funny Girl*,
dressed like *Second Hand Rose*,
always *With a Song in My Heart*.

In my young adult years
I needed an orchestral work to unlock
many feelings trapped inside me.
Rachmaninoff's *Piano Concerto No. 2*
helped me believe in new beginnings,
while Samuel Barber's *Adagio for Strings*
allowed me, as an adolescent, to cry my heart out,
and let go of many broken promises.

Puccini's *La Bohème* introduced passion
and undying romance to my soul.
Morricone's score from the movie *Cinema Paradiso*
taught me to never forget love shared—is precious.

My choral director and mentor, Dorothy DiDomenico,
taught me *Ye shall have a Song* by Randall Thompson
which to this day is tattooed in my soul.

No matter what life
left at my doorstep,
there was always a song
to help me,
a song that understood me,
and made me feel
it was written just for me.

And it all began with birds.
Birds taught me the importance of music and how to begin
and end each day with a song.

Today in my sixties, my mind drifts
on the backs of turtles
to a simpler time in my youth,
now revisited in my golden age wonder.
As I sit by my living room window
looking down at my lake,
hypnotic tinsel waters
dance with the flirting sun.

I sing thanks to my beautiful, imperfect family, rooted in unconditional love.

My eyes moisten with delight every time I watch my strong, vivacious daughter feed and sing to the hundreds of birds who live in her native-garden yard.

I sing thanks to my son-in-law who makes me laugh and not take myself so seriously.

I sing thanks to my son and daughter-in-law who make me proud with their brilliant writing, teaching and love of animals.

I sing thanks to my new husband who supports me in all my endeavors, and grounds me with love and understanding.

I sing thanks to my stepson and his husband— their talents and sensitivity motivate me.

I sing thanks to my dear friend and soul sister Tami who has stood by me for over forty years, and believed in me when I didn't believe in myself.

And I sing thanks to my greatest gifts—my grandsons, who listen to the songs of my heart and let me revisit the world through the eyes of my inner child.

Comfortable in my own Skin

lyrical raindrops
dance through
heavy fog
of my youth

I reflect on
lost buttons
of too much
wear and tear

a life broken in
by an abundance
of uncomfortable
tattered shoes

faded jeans
I wore just yesterday
unable to zip
I try to find a pair that fits

I choose the sweats
of a lifetime
washed memories
softened, cozy

they stretch to my frame
fit me just fine
I am comfortable
with who I am

with whom I am not
as I sit and write
dog by my side
no thought of tomorrow

Tutti

Now I invite your inner student to connect with your divine teacher. This journey can sometimes take a lifetime to achieve. Remember, you have the power to create your own destiny, and produce a teacher based on all the lessons you have learned.

The road is bumpy and at times painful. But if you trust in yourself and let your heart lead the way, you'll find your true voice—that sings to your soul, roots, and secures you to nature's symphonic mastery.

Honor yourself, cherish, and remember your power to connect with all that is good.

Eulogy

Oh, let me leave this world
On eagles' wings
So, I may soar
To the highest mountain
As I look down
On nature's mastery
With songs of millions
Nestled in my heart
Never to be forgotten
As my melody sings on
From here to eternity

About
Michelle Oram

*A*fter graduating from the Boston Conservatory of Music, Michelle explored breath-body mastery and integrated Eastern and Western approaches of yoga, tai-chi, Alexander, and Bel Canto techniques to help her get out of her head and into her heart again. She founded Stagestruck Performing Arts Center where she developed art, dance, drama, musical theatre, and vocal programs for thousands of students from ages three to adult. Many of her students have performed and directed on and off Broadway. Some are composers, vocal coaches, songwriters, dancers, teachers, music therapists and yoga instructors, but all share one thing in common—the importance of music in their daily lives.

After decades in the performing arts, Michelle began her quest as a writer. Perhaps, it was a lifetime of music that inspired her writing to take flight in poetry which has since appeared in many journals and chapbooks including Local Gems Press, NJ, *Bards Northeast Poetry Review* and *The Journal.*

In 2017 she published her first children's book; *Songs of the Woods* encouraging children to begin and end each day with a song from the heart. Michelle composed the accompanying music.

Throughout her journey Michelle has been fortunate to sing with some amazing big bands and jazz ensembles. She hosts Open Mics for Writers and Poets and is breaking new ground with her Jazz Poetry.

When not singing or writing she can be found spending precious moments with her family. Her greatest award in her career is the "Grammy Award" and she is blessed to have two beautiful grandchildren who keep her eyes open to all the magical possibilities life has to offer.

For more info check out her website: **michelleoram.com**

Made in United States
North Haven, CT
30 May 2024

53081048R10089